take
good care

take
good care

illustrated by mary engelbreit

written by patrick regan

**Andrews McMeel
Publishing**

Kansas City

www.maryengelbreit.com

and Mary Engelbreit are registered trademarks of
Mary Engelbreit Enterprises, Inc.

03 04 05 06 07 EPB 10 9 8 7 6 5 4 3 2 1

Design by Stephanie R. Farley and Delsie Chambon

ISBN: 0-7407-3906-9

The greatest
healing therapy
is friendship
and love.

— Hubert Humphrey

Being sick is the pits...
There's no point
in denying.
It's no fun to be
stuck in bed.

While the rest of the world
    Seems to roll right along,
You're alone,
    feeling lousy instead.

But you're *not* all alone
If you have friends
to cheer you—
And that's something
you'll never lack.

And though you feel yucky,
We all still feel lucky
To count you as
one of our pack.

'Cause when
you're around,
Life is somehow
more lively,

And the days seem
a little more bright.

With a smile
that's contagious

And a laugh
that's outrageous,

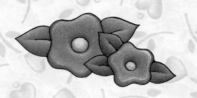

You make even tough times
seem all right.

So don't let this setback
Squash your sense
of humor,
Keep smiling through
this sinking spell.

Get plenty of rest,
Heed what doctors
suggest,

And do what you need
to get well!

And when you feel better,
We'll get back to business—
The business of
        just having fun.

We'll gab
without stopping,

Drink tea and
go shopping...
There's so much
that needs to be done!

Though you're
    under the weather
We'll stick close together
  Till gray skies become
    brilliant blue

And when the clouds
have all passed
You'll see tough times
don't last,

But friendships
like ours
surely do.

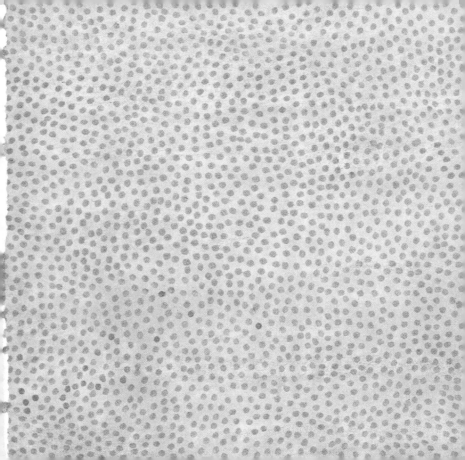